Twenty-Minute
Chicken Dishes

K A R E N   A .   L E V I N

CONTEMPORARY BOOKS

Library of Congress Cataloging-in-Publication Data

Levin, Karen.
 Twenty-minute chicken dishes : delicious, easy-to-prepare
meals everyone will love / Karen A. Levin.
  p.   cm.
 Includes index.
 ISBN 0-8092-4033-5
  1. Cookery (Chicken)   2. Quick and easy cookery.
I. Title.
TX750.5.C45L48   1991
641.6'65—dc20   91-3916
                                                      CIP

To my loving and loyal family of recipe tasters:
my husband, Robert, and our children, Amelia and Andrew

Contents

3 ETHNIC DISHES   47

1
INTRODUCTION

American eating habits have changed dramatically in the last ten years. Often, the tradition of spending hours preparing the evening meal is just no longer possible. For those who still cherish the joy of cooking at home, of filling the house with wonderful smells, this book will provide the means to that valuable end.

Although take-out meals, convenience foods, and fast-food chains are admittedly easy and expeditious, they are also expensive and lack variety. The recipes in this book are cheaper to make, healthier to eat, and much more flavorful than prepared foods. Best of all, each of the recipes in this book can be prepared in twenty minutes from start to finish, and you need not be a master chef to meet the twenty-minute deadline. All that is required are planning and concentration. The result will be a rewarding and satisfying home-cooked meal.

Timing

The first step in preparing a quick meal is to take a few minutes to read over the recipe, plan the course of action, and get out all the ingredients and utensils before beginning. Concentration is the key. If you are using an electric range top, plan to start heating the skillet early. Preheat the broiler or grill at the onset of preparation for those recipes that call for broiling or grilling. I find it helpful to be thinking ahead to the next preparation step as I am working.

You'll see that a preparation time is noted at the beginning of each recipe. That is the time it will take to get things started. After the chicken begins cooking, there may be additional preparation of ingredients for a sauce or topping that can be done while the chicken is cooking.

Purchasing Chicken

Needless to say, almost all of the recipes call for the fastest-cooking and most versatile cut of chicken: boneless breasts or thighs. To my amazement, I have found that most butchers, whether in supermarkets or small butcher shops, do not mind boning chicken thighs at no additional cost. Some even say they prefer to bone the thighs because it is much easier than boning the breasts. Prepackaged boneless thighs recently have begun to appear in large supermarkets across the country.

Many of the stir-fry dishes and stews in this book call for "chicken tenders" or boneless chicken breasts or thighs, cut into pieces. Chicken tenders are the tenderloin muscles from the breasts. These are usually available in supermarkets. Also available are chicken breasts precut into strips for stir-frying. Both the chicken tenders and stir-fry chicken are expensive, though, so I have allowed for the cutting of boneless breasts or thighs as part of the preparation time. You can make this task easier by cutting the chicken while it is still partially frozen.

It's a good idea to put chicken at the top of your shopping list and visit the meat department first. If the type of chicken you want is not available in the meat case, ask the butcher to prepare it for you while you do the rest of your shopping.

Note that the recipes call for *whole* chicken breasts, split. A normal serving of chicken is a 4-ounce breast *half*. For example, two whole chicken breasts, split, boned, and skinned, will yield 4 pieces of chicken for 4 servings. Most often, the chicken breasts already will be split for you by the butcher.

For those of you who are handy at boning your own chicken breasts, there is even more money to be saved. I use the weekend to bone and freeze chicken and use the bones to make chicken broth.

Safety and Storage

As with any meat product, raw chicken requires careful attention when handling. The National Broiler Council recommends these practical guidelines:

- Refrigerate raw chicken promptly after it is purchased. Tray-packed chicken can be refrigerated up to 2 days in its original wrapping.
- For longer storage, freeze raw or precooked chicken in moistureproof freezer paper or freezer storage plastic bags, securely sealed with the air pressed out. Frozen raw chicken should be used within 6 months. Frozen cooked chicken should be used within 2 months.
- Thaw frozen chicken in the refrigerator, microwave oven, or under cold running water, but never at room temperature.
- Wash chicken in cool water; pat dry with a paper towel before preparing for cooking.
- Wash hands, work surfaces, knives, and utensils thoroughly in hot, soapy water immediately after handling raw chicken.

- Never place cooked chicken on the same plate or tray used for raw chicken without first washing the plate thoroughly.
- Store cooked chicken for picnics in an insulated container or ice chest; keep refrigerated until ready to eat.
- Always cook chicken until it is well-done (160°F). Boneless chicken will feel firm and somewhat springy when it is done. Juices should run clear, not pink, when the chicken is cut at the thickest portion.
- Cooked chicken that is not eaten immediately should be kept either hot (140°F to 165°F) or refrigerated (40°F or less). Do not leave at room temperature for more than 2 hours.

To Skin or Not to Skin?

That is the question! It is true that almost all the fat and cholesterol in chicken is found in the skin. Still, the skin bastes the chicken during dry-heat methods of cooking such as grilling and broiling and gives the meat a marvelous flavor. Many of these recipes call for skinless chicken. Others, however, state, "skinned if desired." If you are following a low-fat, low-cholesterol diet you may want to skin the chicken (or purchase it skinned) before cooking. Otherwise, cook the chicken with the skin on and then decide whether or not to discard the skin before serving.

Ingredients

These recipes call for a minimum amount of added fat. The amount of salt called for in the recipes is to bring out the flavor of the dish, but it can be easily omitted for those following low-sodium diets. Mustard appears in many of the recipes because it provides a wealth of flavor. For those on low-sodium diets, look for no-salt-added mustard in the health food section of the supermarket.

You will find that onion and garlic form the base for many of the sauces. No other staple ingredients give so much rich flavor for so little preparation time. Peeling and chopping an onion by hand should become second nature to the home cook. As many times as I have tried the onion and garlic pastes, powders, and salts, I have yet to feel they are an adequate substitute for the real thing. These recipes allow for time to do the hand chopping. If you own a food processor or mini food processor, mince the garlic first and then add the onion and process until chopped. The preparation time saved will be spent during cleanup, but many cooks prefer this trade-off.

Serving Sizes

The recipes in this book were developed to serve four but may easily be halved or doubled. When halving the recipes with sauces, use an 8-inch skillet rather than the standard large, 10-inch skillet. When doubling these recipes, use a 10-inch sauté (straight-sided) pan or a 12-inch skillet. All of the stews and one-dish meals freeze extremely well. You may wish to make double batches of these for future meals.

A Word About Pounding

To ensure quicker and more even cooking, boneless chicken breasts can be pounded to an even (usually ½-inch) thickness. Frequently, purchased chicken breasts are already evened out during the boning process. Many of these recipes, therefore, do not call for pounding. Where it is critical to the timing of the recipe, however, I have included this step.

There are a multitude of ways in which to pound chicken. The easiest method I have found is to place the chicken between sheets of plastic wrap or leave it in the freezer wrap or freezer storage plastic bag in which it was thawed. Starting in the center, pound the breast with the palm of your hand, a heavy-bottomed skillet, or the flat edge of a meat mallet. (I have even used the side of a can of tomatoes.) The process should not take more than 1 minute to complete and will save several minutes of cooking time.

2
REGIONAL AMERICAN DISHES

Americans' growing preference for chicken can be understood on many levels. Perhaps most fundamental is the desire for a healthier alternative to red meat. On another level, chicken is less expensive. With a minimum of ingenuity, one can create a satisfying chicken dish. But Americans have moved beyond these basics to a point where the diversity of preparations reflect the melting pot of American culture. Each region of the country seems to have its favorite chicken recipe, utilizing available ingredients or combinations of ingredients and epitomizing the uniqueness of the region.

CHICKEN WITH ROASTED RED PEPPER SAUCE

The trend for roasting bell peppers began in California restaurants when the popular peppers became available in abundant supply. The flavor of roasted red and yellow peppers is wonderful, but the process can be time-consuming. Now that bottled roasted red (and even yellow) peppers are a common supermarket ingredient, this dish can be prepared in no time at all.

Preparation time: 4 minutes
Cooking time: 14 minutes
Makes 4 servings

2 whole chicken breasts, split and boned (skinned, if desired)
¾ teaspoon salt, divided
¼ teaspoon freshly ground black pepper
2 tablespoons butter or margarine
2 cloves garlic, minced
1 7-ounce jar roasted red or yellow bell peppers, drained
¼ cup sour cream or crème fraîche
2 tablespoons prepared salsa or picante sauce
1 teaspoon flour
2 tablespoons chopped fresh basil, cilantro, or parsley

Pound chicken to ½-inch thickness. Sprinkle with ½ teaspoon of the salt and pepper. Heat butter in a large skillet over medium-high heat. Add chicken and garlic and cook 4 to 5 minutes per side or until chicken is cooked through. While chicken is cooking, pat peppers dry with paper towels. Puree in a blender or food processor until fairly smooth. Add sour cream, salsa, flour, and remaining ¼ teaspoon salt. Blend until fairly smooth. Remove chicken to a serving platter. Add pepper mixture to skillet and cook 1 to 2 minutes or until thickened, stirring constantly. Spoon over chicken and sprinkle with basil.

Serving suggestions: Serve with a mixed green salad and pita or bagel chips.

CHICKEN IN CREAMY AVOCADO SAUCE

▪▬▪▬▪▬▪▬▪▬▪▬▪▬▪▬▪▬▪

Haas avocados from California are dark in color with a pebbly skin and a creamy, rich texture. Fuerte avocados from Florida are light green with a smooth skin and contain more water. The Haas variety is preferred for this dish.

Preparation time: 5 minutes
Cooking time: 12 minutes
Makes 4 servings

2 whole chicken breasts, split, boned, and skinned
1 tablespoon olive oil
1½ teaspoons ground cumin
½ teaspoon salt
¼–½ teaspoon cayenne pepper, as desired
2 cloves garlic, minced
1 8-ounce can stewed tomatoes
⅓ cup sour cream
1 ripe avocado, peeled, seeded, and diced
¼ cup coarsely chopped cilantro

Pound chicken to ½-inch thickness. Heat oil in a large skillet. Sprinkle chicken with cumin, salt, and cayenne pepper. Place chicken and garlic in skillet and cook over medium-high heat, 2 minutes per side. Add tomatoes; cover and simmer until chicken is cooked through, 5 to 6 minutes. Transfer chicken to a serving platter; keep warm. Cook juices in skillet over high heat until thickened, about 2 minutes. Reduce heat to low; stir in sour cream, avocado, and cilantro until well blended. Pour over chicken.

Serving suggestions: Serve over hot cooked linguine with a salad of orange sections and julienned jicama in a dressing of lime juice, chili powder, and olive oil.

HONEY-LIME CHICKEN

Florida is famous for its abundant citrus crop. This dish pairs the gentle sweet-sour flavor combination of honey and lime. The chicken cooks unwatched in the oven while you prepare the rest of the meal.

Preparation time: 3 minutes
Cooking time: 17 minutes
Makes 4 servings

⅓ cup honey
2 tablespoons fresh lime juice
1½ tablespoons soy sauce
2 whole chicken breasts, split and boned (skinned, if
    desired)

Preheat oven to 450°F. Combine honey, lime juice, and soy sauce in a shallow ovenproof casserole dish large enough to hold chicken in one layer. Add chicken and turn to coat. Turn skin-side up and bake 10 minutes. Baste chicken with juices in casserole dish and continue to bake until chicken is cooked through, about 7 minutes. Transfer chicken to a serving platter and spoon juices over chicken.

Serving suggestions: Serve with couscous and a steamed green vegetable.

GILROY GARLIC CHICKEN WITH BASIL, MINT, AND LEMON

Gilroy, California, is the garlic capital of the world. Its annual garlic festival brings garlic lovers from all over America. This dish was inspired by the abundance of fresh herbs that is also a California resource.

Preparation time: 15 minutes
Cooking time: 5 minutes
Makes 4 servings

1 pound boneless, skinless chicken breasts or chicken tenders
3 cloves garlic, minced
¾ teaspoon salt
2 tablespoons olive oil
1 7-ounce jar or ½ cup roasted red peppers, drained and sliced
½ cup packed fresh basil leaves, stems removed
2 tablespoons chopped fresh mint leaves
1 tablespoon fresh lemon juice (see Note)
Freshly ground black pepper to taste

Cut chicken into 1-inch pieces; toss with garlic and salt. Heat oil in a large skillet over high heat. Add chicken mixture; stir-fry until chicken is cooked through, about 4 minutes. Add red peppers, basil, mint, and lemon juice; cook and stir 1 minute or until peppers are heated through and basil is wilted. Sprinkle generously with pepper.

Note: For a fresher and more intense lemon flavor, finely grate ½ teaspoon of lemon peel and sprinkle over the finished dish. This will require an extra minute of preparation time but will also provide a pretty garnish.

Serving suggestions: Serve with baked or fried goat cheese and crusty Italian rolls or bread sticks.

GRILLED CHICKEN VINAIGRETTE ON MIXED BITTER GREENS

This dish was inspired by a similar dish I had in San Diego, California.

Preparation time: 6 minutes
Cooking time: 10 minutes
Makes 4 servings

3 tablespoons balsamic or good quality red-wine vinegar
1 tablespoon Dijon-style mustard
2 cloves garlic, minced
½ teaspoon freshly ground black pepper
⅓ cup good quality olive oil
2 whole chicken breasts, split and boned (skinned if desired)
5 cups packed mixed torn greens such as chicory, arugula, mâche, red leaf, oak leaf, spinach, romaine, or Belgian endive
2 tablespoons freshly grated Asiago, Parmesan, or Romano cheese

Combine vinegar, mustard, garlic, and pepper; whisk in oil until thickened. Reserve ¼ cup of the dressing; spread remaining dressing over both sides of chicken. Grill or broil chicken 4 to 5 inches from heat source until cooked through, about 5 minutes per side. Meanwhile, toss greens with remaining dressing. Slice chicken crosswise into thin strips; arrange over greens. Sprinkle with cheese and serve with additional black pepper, if desired.

Serving suggestions: Serve with whole-grain bread with sweet butter and your favorite broth-based soup.

ARIZONA CHICKEN IN SPICY LIME SAUCE

The use of assertive flavors helps keep ingredients to a minimum in this Southwestern dish.

Preparation time: 4 minutes
Cooking time: 12 minutes
Makes 4 servings

2 whole chicken breasts, split, boned, and skinned
1 tablespoon Dijon-style mustard
1 tablespoon butter or margarine
½ cup prepared salsa or picante sauce
2 tablespoons fresh lime juice
¼ cup coarsely chopped cilantro

Pound chicken to ½-inch thickness; spread with mustard. Heat butter in a large skillet. Add chicken and cook over medium-high heat 2 minutes per side. Combine salsa and lime juice; add to skillet. Simmer uncovered until chicken is cooked through and sauce has thickened, 6 to 8 minutes. Sprinkle with cilantro.

Serving suggestions: Serve with warm corn tortillas and instant grits with sour cream and Monterey Jack cheese stirred in after cooking.

CHICKEN SALAD CAESAR

The classic Caesar salad was created in Tijuana, Mexico, in 1924, but it has become one of the most popular salads in America. Adding chicken turns the salad into a main course and creates a palate-pleasing hot-and-cold texture.

Preparation time: 10 minutes
Cooking time: 6 minutes
Makes 4 servings

1 pound skinless, boneless chicken breasts or chicken tenders
½ teaspoon salt
¼ teaspoon freshly ground black pepper
¼ cup olive oil
3 cloves garlic, minced
4 cups torn romaine lettuce
2 tablespoons fresh lemon juice
1 cup purchased or homemade garlic croutons
¼ cup (1 ounce) grated Parmesan cheese
8 anchovy fillets (optional)

Cut chicken into 1-inch by ¼-inch strips and sprinkle with salt and pepper. Heat oil in a large skillet over medium-high heat. Add chicken and garlic and cook until chicken is cooked through, stirring frequently, about 5 minutes. While chicken is cooking, arrange lettuce in a large, shallow bowl. Add chicken mixture and lemon juice. Add croutons and cheese and toss well. Transfer to four plates and garnish with anchovies and additional cheese, if desired.

Serving suggestions: Serve with buttered baby peas and oven-roasted potato fingers brushed with olive oil and rosemary.

NEW MEXICO GRILLED CHICKEN WITH CILANTRO OIL

Cilantro has become an increasingly popular herb in this country. There is no substitute for its pungent, peppery taste. It is the trademark herb of Southwestern cooking.

Preparation time: 3 minutes
Cooking time: 10 minutes
Makes 4 servings

2 whole chicken breasts, split and boned (skinned if desired)
Salt and cayenne pepper to taste
1–2 tablespoons olive or vegetable oil
½ cup cilantro leaves without stems
1 clove garlic, peeled
¼ cup good quality olive oil

Sprinkle chicken with salt and cayenne pepper to taste; brush lightly with oil. Grill or broil 4 to 5 inches from heat source until cooked through, about 5 minutes per side. While chicken is cooking, place cilantro and garlic in a food processor or blender; process until finely chopped. With the motor running, add ¼ cup oil in a stream; process until well mixed. Drizzle over hot grilled chicken.

Serving suggestions: Slice small zucchini lengthwise; brush with olive oil and sprinkle with salt and pepper. Grill or broil alongside chicken and drizzle with some of the cilantro oil. Serve with warm flour or corn tortillas.

CORNMEAL CHICKEN SAUTE

Abundant and flavorful cornmeal has long been neglected as a wonderful foodstuff. Here, the cornmeal coating keeps the chicken extremely moist and tender and enriches the flavor.

Preparation time: 10 minutes
Cooking time: 10 minutes
Makes 4 servings

2 whole chicken breasts, split, boned, and skinned
1 tablespoon flour
1 egg
⅓ cup cornmeal
1 teaspoon ground cumin
¾ teaspoon salt
¼ teaspoon cayenne pepper
3 tablespoons vegetable oil
1 small ripe avocado, peeled, seeded, and sliced
Approximately ⅓ cup sour cream or yogurt as garnish
Approximately ¼ cup prepared salsa or picante sauce as garnish

Pound chicken to ½-inch thickness. Place flour in a plastic bag. Beat egg in a shallow plate or pie plate. Combine cornmeal, cumin, salt, and cayenne pepper in another shallow plate. Place chicken, 2 pieces at a time, in bag with flour and shake to coat. Remove chicken from bag and dip in egg. Roll in cornmeal mixture, pressing to coat. Heat oil in a large skillet over medium-high heat. Add chicken and cook until browned and cooked through, about 5 minutes per side. Place on a serving platter; top with avocado, sour cream, and salsa.

Serving suggestions: Serve with canned refried beans doctored with salsa and sliced green onions and a tossed green salad.

TEX-MEX CHICKEN CHILI

Prepared jalapeño relish varies in heat by brand. Salsa and picante sauce have variable heat levels labeled mild, medium, or hot. Choose a heat level that enables you to comfortably experience this delicious blend of North American cultures.

Preparation time: 7 minutes
Cooking time: 13 minutes
Makes 4 servings

1 tablespoon olive or vegetable oil
1 pound boneless, skinless chicken breasts or thighs, cut into 1½-inch pieces
1 tablespoon ground cumin
1 tablespoon chili powder
1 large yellow onion, coarsely chopped
2 cloves garlic, minced
1 14- to 16-ounce can stewed tomatoes or Mexican stewed tomatoes
1 16-ounce can black beans, drained
¼ cup jalapeño relish *or* ½ cup prepared salsa or picante sauce
½ teaspoon salt
¼ cup chopped cilantro as garnish
¼ cup sour cream as garnish

Heat oil in a large skillet over medium-high heat. Add chicken; sprinkle with cumin and chili powder. Cook 1 minute, stirring constantly. Add onion and garlic; cook 1 minute. Add tomatoes, beans, relish or salsa, and salt. Bring to a boil. Reduce heat; simmer uncovered 10 minutes or until chicken is cooked through. Ladle into bowls; top with cilantro and sour cream.

Serving suggestions: Serve with blue corn or regular tortilla chips and sliced avocado and tomato salad with red wine vinaigrette dressing.

BARBECUED CHICKEN

Traditional barbecued chicken does not have to take hours to prepare, as this delicious recipe demonstrates. The sauce can be covered and refrigerated for up to three weeks.

Preparation time: 4 minutes
Cooking time: 10–16 minutes
Makes 4 servings

¼ cup catsup
2 tablespoons brown sugar
1 tablespoon Worcestershire sauce
1 tablespoon light soy sauce
2 whole chicken breasts, split and boned (skinned if desired) *or* 2 pounds chicken wings and small legs (drumstick portion)

Combine catsup, brown sugar, Worcestershire sauce, and soy sauce; mix well. Grill or broil chicken 4 to 5 inches from heat source, brushing often with sauce, until chicken is cooked through, about 5 minutes per side for boneless breasts, 8 minutes per side for wings and legs.

Serving suggestions: Serve with coleslaw, pickles, hot peppers, and baked beans.

BUFFALO CHICKEN WINGS

This traditional recipe from its namesake city in New York is extremely hot. For a milder version, cut the hot pepper sauce to 2 teaspoons. The deep-frying step has been eliminated and replaced with a much quicker broiling method. Drumettes are the meaty portion of the chicken wings and usually come prepackaged in the meat case of most supermarkets. If unavailable, purchase 6 chicken wings and disjoint them, discarding the wing tips.

Preparation time: 9 minutes
Cooking time: 11 minutes
Makes 2 main dish or 4 appetizer servings

2 tablespoons mayonnaise or light mayonnaise
1 tablespoon hot pepper sauce
½ cup seasoned bread crumbs
12 chicken drumettes (about 1 pound)

Combine mayonnaise and pepper sauce in a small bowl. Place bread crumbs in another small bowl. Dip chicken drumettes in mayonnaise mixture, or use a rubber spatula to spread mixture evenly over chicken. Roll in bread crumbs and place on the rack of a broiler pan. Broil 4 to 5 inches from heat source for 5 minutes. Turn and continue to broil until chicken is cooked through and crumbs are deep golden brown, 5 to 6 minutes.

Serving suggestions: This dish is typically served with blue cheese dressing for dipping and celery sticks to help cool the heat of the hot sauce.

ONION-SMOTHERED CHICKEN

This dish calls for sweet onions, which include Vidalia, Texas 1015, Walla Walla, and Maui. At least one of these varieties is usually available from late April to August. If sweet onions are unavailable, substitute Spanish onions.

Preparation time: 5 minutes
Cooking time: 15 minutes
Makes 4 servings

1 pound boneless, skinless chicken breasts or thighs
1 tablespoon prepared honey mustard
1 tablespoon butter
1 tablespoon olive oil
1 large sweet onion, thinly sliced
¼ teaspoon salt
¼ teaspoon freshly ground black pepper

Pound chicken to ½-inch thickness; spread evenly with honey mustard. Heat butter and oil in a large skillet over medium-high heat. Add chicken; cook 3 minutes. Turn; separate onion slices into rings and scatter over chicken. Reduce heat to medium; cover and cook until chicken is cooked through, about 8 minutes. Remove chicken to a serving platter with a slotted spatula, leaving onions in skillet. Increase heat to high; add salt and pepper to onions. Cook until onions are soft and glazed, about 4 minutes, stirring frequently. Spoon over chicken.

Note: Prepared honey mustard has a thicker consistency that works best for this recipe, but a good substitute is equal parts of grainy Dijon-style mustard and honey. This version is best used as a dipping sauce for cooked chicken, not coating.

Serving suggestions: Serve with a crisp vegetable salad and garlic toast.

SOUTHERN FRIED CHICKEN IN PEPPER-CREAM GRAVY

This dish offers true down-home flavors of typical South-ern-style fried chicken in only one third the time. Southern-ers are fond of enormous quantities of black pepper, but you may use your own judgment in accordance with your taste.

Preparation time: 7 minutes
Cooking time: 13 minutes
Makes 4 servings

2 whole chicken breasts, split and boned (skinned if desired)
⅓ cup buttermilk
½ teaspoon hot pepper sauce
½ cup plus 1 tablespoon flour
1¼ teaspoons salt
¼ cup vegetable oil
¾ cup milk
¼–½ teaspoon freshly ground black pepper, as desired

Pound chicken to ½-inch thickness. Combine buttermilk and pepper sauce in a shallow plate or pie plate. Combine ½ cup of the flour and salt in another shallow plate. Add chicken to buttermilk mixture; turn to coat. Roll in flour mixture to coat lightly. Heat oil in a heavy, large skillet over medium-high heat. Fry chicken in oil 4 minutes or until golden brown; reduce heat to medium. Turn chicken and fry until cooked through, about 5 minutes. Remove to paper towels to drain. Add remaining 1 tablespoon flour to skillet; cook and stir 1 minute. Add milk and pepper; cook and stir until thickened; pour over chicken.

Serving suggestions: Serve with fresh corn on the cob, buttermilk biscuits, and instant whipped potatoes drizzled with some of the pepper cream gravy.

CHICKEN PECAN

Pecans are plentiful in the South, and this dish uses them to great advantage. Southerners use margarine more often than butter. If you are using butter, take care not to burn the coating.

Preparation time: 8 minutes
Cooking time: 10 minutes
Makes 4 servings

2 whole chicken breasts, split, boned, and skinned
Salt and freshly ground black pepper to taste
1½ tablespoons Dijon-style mustard
⅓ cup finely chopped pecans
⅓ cup fresh bread crumbs (see Note)
2–3 tablespoons margarine or butter, as needed

Pound chicken to ½-inch thickness. Sprinkle with salt and pepper to taste. Spread mustard evenly over both sides of chicken. Combine pecans and bread crumbs in a shallow dish. Roll chicken in pecan and bread crumb mixture until lightly coated. Cook in margarine in a large skillet over medium heat until browned and cooked through, about 5 minutes per side.

Note: To make fresh bread crumbs, process torn sliced bread in a food processor or blender.

Serving suggestions: Serve with whipped potatoes with a dash of horseradish stirred in and carrots cooked in apple cider with a dash of cinnamon.

CAJUN GRILLED CHICKEN

Louisiana spices enliven this simple, grilled chicken breast. For a hotter dish, increase the amount of cayenne pepper used.

Preparation time: 7 minutes
Cooking time: 10 minutes
Makes 4 servings

2 whole chicken breasts, boned and split (skinned, if
   desired)
2 tablespoons olive oil
2 cloves garlic, minced
1½ teaspoons dried thyme
½ teaspoon salt
½ teaspoon cayenne pepper
¼ teaspoon ground white pepper
¼ teaspoon freshly ground black pepper

Pound chicken to ½-inch thickness. Combine remaining ingredients; brush evenly over chicken. Grill or broil 4 to 5 inches from heat source until chicken is cooked through, about 5 minutes per side.

Serving suggestions: Serve with a fresh spinach and red onion salad with poppy seed dressing and corn on the cob when in season or buttered frozen corn kernels when out of season.

CHICKEN GUMBO

Cajun seasonings add a depth of flavor to quick-cooking foods. Both filé (pronounced FEE-lay) powder and Cajun or creole seasonings are available in the spice section of most supermarkets. Prepared blends vary, but most contain a mixture of thyme, oregano, garlic salt or powder, onion powder, cayenne pepper, and ground white and black peppers. Filé powder gives the dish an authentic flavor, but if it's unavailable, it may be omitted.

Preparation time: 6 minutes
Cooking time: 14 minutes
Makes 4 servings

4 slices bacon, diced
1 large yellow onion, coarsely chopped
2 tablespoons flour
1 pound skinless, boneless chicken thighs, cut into
    1½-inch pieces
1 large green bell pepper, coarsely chopped
1 14- to 16-ounce can stewed tomatoes or Cajun stewed
    tomatoes
1 cup chicken broth
2 bay leaves
2–3 teaspoons Cajun or creole seasoning, as desired
1 teaspoon gumbo filé powder
Approximately 2 tablespoons chopped fresh parsley
    (optional)

Cook bacon and onion in a large skillet over medium-high heat for 3 minutes. Sprinkle evenly with flour; cook and stir 1 minute. Add chicken and green pepper; cook 1 minute, stirring constantly. Add remaining ingredients except filé powder and parsley; cover and simmer 8 minutes or until chicken is cooked through and sauce has thickened. Remove bay leaves. Stir in filé powder; remove from heat. Ladle into bowls and sprinkle with parsley, if desired.

Serving suggestions: Add a spoonful of hot cooked white or brown rice to each serving of gumbo. Serve with pita chips or bread sticks.

CHICKEN JAMBALAYA

Jambalaya, another favorite Cajun dish, is similar to a gumbo but does not have a flour-thickened base. Andouille or creole sausage is a spicy hot sausage found in large supermarkets or specialty stores. If it is unavailable, substitute smoked sausage and add more hot pepper sauce to taste.

Preparation time: 2 minutes
Cooking time: 18 minutes
Makes 6 servings

½ pound andouille or creole sausage, sliced ½-inch thick
½ pound boneless, skinless chicken breasts, thighs, or chicken tenders
½ teaspoon salt
½–1 teaspoon hot pepper sauce, as desired
1 cup thinly sliced celery
1 medium yellow onion, coarsely chopped
2 cloves garlic, minced
2 14-ounce cans stewed tomatoes or Cajun stewed tomatoes
1 bay leaf
2 cups cooked white rice
¼ cup chopped fresh parsley

Cook sausage in a large skillet over medium heat for 2 minutes. While sausage is cooking, cut chicken into 1-inch pieces; sprinkle with salt and pepper sauce. Add to skillet with celery, onion, and garlic. Cook until chicken is no longer pink, about 3 minutes, stirring frequently. Add tomatoes and bay leaf; bring to a boil. Cover and simmer 8 to 10 minutes or until chicken is cooked through. Stir in rice; heat through. Remove bay leaf; ladle into bowls and sprinkle with parsley.

Serving suggestions: Serve with warmed sourdough or rye bread and a mixed salad of bitter greens.

QUICK CHICKEN NOODLE SOUP

This soup is so flavorful and fast that you may never open a can of chicken noodle soup again.

Preparation time: 8 minutes
Cooking time: 12 minutes
Makes 4 servings

1 tablespoon butter or margarine
2 small carrots, thinly sliced
1 small yellow onion, chopped
1 clove garlic, minced
½ pound boneless, skinless chicken breasts, thighs, or chicken tenders
Salt and freshly ground black pepper to taste
2 14-ounce cans chicken broth
2 ounces very thin egg noodles, uncooked (about 1 cup)
¼ cup chopped celery leaves or parsley (optional)

Heat butter in a large saucepan over medium-high heat. Add carrots, onion, and garlic and cook 3 minutes, stirring occasionally. While vegetables are cooking, cut chicken into ½-inch pieces. Add to saucepan and sprinkle with salt and pepper to taste. Cook 1 minute, stirring constantly. Add broth and noodles. Cover and bring to a boil. Reduce heat to medium-low. Simmer, covered, 8 to 9 minutes or until noodles are tender and chicken is cooked through. Stir in celery leaves, if desired.

Serving suggestions: Serve with an assortment of crackers or with garlic toast for a satisfying lunch. For a main dish supper, serve with a chef's salad and crusty French bread or hard rolls.

FRUITED CHICKEN

Fall brings an abundance of crisp, sweet apples, mainly from the state of Washington. Courtland, Jonathan, and McIntosh are good choices for this easy stir-fry dish.

Preparation time: 12 minutes
Cooking time: 6 minutes
Makes 4 servings

½ cup unsweetened apple juice
¼ cup port wine
1 tablespoon cornstarch
1 pound chicken tenders or boneless, skinless chicken breasts, cut into 1-inch pieces
1 teaspoon salt
½ teaspoon paprika
½ teaspoon cinnamon
1 large red apple, unpeeled
2 tablespoons vegetable oil
¼ cup coarsely chopped toasted walnuts

Combine juice, wine, and cornstarch; set aside. Sprinkle chicken with salt, paprika, and cinnamon; toss to coat. Cut apple into ½-inch chunks; set aside. Heat oil in a large skillet or wok over medium-high heat. Add seasoned chicken and stir-fry until it is no longer pink, about 2 minutes. Add apple and stir-fry until chicken is cooked through, about 2 minutes. Add juice mixture. Cook, stirring constantly, until sauce has thickened, about 1 minute. Stir in walnuts.

Serving suggestions: Serve over hot brown rice or egg noodles with a spinach and romaine lettuce salad.

CASCADE CHICKEN WITH EXOTIC MUSHROOMS

Fresh exotic mushrooms have become increasingly available in large supermarkets and specialty produce markets. Shiitake mushrooms are earthy tasting, while oyster mushrooms are light and delicate. Crimini mushrooms have a more robust flavor than white mushrooms. For an even more special dish, use a mixture of three kinds.

Preparation time: 5 minutes
Cooking time: 15 minutes
Makes 4 servings

2 whole chicken breasts, split, boned, and skinned
¾ teaspoon salt
¼ teaspoon freshly ground black pepper
2 tablespoons butter or margarine
3–4 ounces fresh shiitake mushrooms, stems discarded, caps thickly sliced
3–4 ounces fresh oyster, crimini, or white mushrooms, halved if large
¼ teaspoon crushed dried rosemary
3 tablespoons dry madeira wine or brandy
⅓ cup whipping cream
2 tablespoons chopped fresh chives or thinly sliced green onion

Pound chicken to ½-inch thickness. Sprinkle with salt and pepper. Heat butter in a large skillet. Add chicken and cook over medium-high heat until chicken is lightly browned on one side, about 4 minutes. Turn; sprinkle with mushrooms and rosemary. Continue cooking until chicken is cooked through, about 6 minutes. Transfer chicken to a serving platter, leaving mushrooms in skillet. Add wine to skillet; increase heat to high and cook 1 minute. Add cream to skillet; cook and stir until sauce is desired consistency, 3 to 4 minutes. Pour over chicken; sprinkle with chives.

Serving suggestions: Serve with tricolor rotini pasta and steamed brussels sprouts or green beans.

NEW YORK BISTRO CHICKEN

This version of sautéed Bistro chicken cuts the 1 hour roasting time of the traditional recipe to 20 minutes—with all the flavor still intact. Serving the chicken with French bread is a must. Spread the bread with some of the softened garlic cloves and flavorful olive oil from the skillet.

Preparation time: 5 minutes
Cooking time: 15 minutes
Makes 4 servings

3 tablespoons olive oil
1 head fresh garlic, separated into unpeeled cloves
2 whole chicken breasts, split and boned (skinned if desired)
1 teaspoon dried thyme
½ teaspoon crushed dried rosemary leaves
½ teaspoon salt
½ teaspoon freshly ground black pepper

Combine oil and garlic in a large skillet. Cover and cook over medium heat for 5 minutes. Meanwhile, pound chicken to ½-inch thickness. Sprinkle evenly with seasonings. Uncover skillet; stir garlic and push to edge of skillet. Add chicken; cook 4 to 5 minutes per side or until chicken is cooked through. Remove garlic with a slotted spoon. Squeeze softened garlic out of peel over chicken, discarding garlic peels. Transfer chicken and garlic to a serving platter and drizzle with skillet juices.

Serving suggestions: Serve with a salad of roasted red, yellow, and green bell peppers and goat cheese with fresh basil and crusty French bread.

CHICKEN CLUB SANDWICH

Nothing beats the traditional flavor combination in the classic club sandwich. In this dish, chicken replaces turkey for a quick and satisfying main dish supper.

Preparation time: 1 minute
Cooking time: 19 minutes
Makes 4 servings

4 slices bacon, cut in half
1 small yellow onion *or* 2 large shallots
2 whole chicken breasts, split and boned (skinned if desired)
1 tablespoon coarse-grained Dijon-style mustard
1 medium tomato
4 large slices sourdough bread, toasted
Freshly ground black pepper to taste

Cook bacon in a large skillet over medium-high heat, turning once, until crisp, about 7 minutes. Remove to paper towels to drain. While bacon is cooking, slice onion thinly and separate into rings. Cook onion in bacon drippings 1 to 2 minutes or until softened. Spread chicken evenly on both sides with mustard. Push onion rings to edge of skillet and add chicken. Cook until chicken is cooked through, 4 to 5 minutes per side. While chicken is cooking, seed and dice tomato and set aside. Remove chicken and onion with a slotted spatula and place over toast. Top with bacon and tomato and sprinkle with pepper.

Serving suggestions: Serve with celery and carrot sticks and coleslaw or potato salad.

NEW ENGLAND CHICKEN IN BRANDIED CHEESE SAUCE

This rich, delicious dish is perfect for entertaining.

Preparation time: 5 minutes
Cooking time: 14 minutes
Makes 4 servings

2 whole chicken breasts, split, boned, and skinned
Salt and freshly ground black pepper to taste
2 tablespoons butter or margarine
1 small yellow onion, finely chopped
¼ cup cognac or brandy
¼ cup chicken broth
1 3-ounce package cream cheese, cubed

Sprinkle chicken with salt and pepper to taste. Heat butter in a large skillet. Add chicken and onion and cook over medium-high heat until chicken is cooked through, about 5 minutes per side, stirring onion occasionally. Transfer chicken to a warm serving plate. Add cognac to skillet; cook 1 minute. Add broth and cheese; cook and stir until cheese is melted and sauce has thickened, about 3 minutes. Spoon over chicken; sprinkle with additional freshly ground black pepper.

Serving suggestions: Serve with fresh tomato or carrot pasta and sautéed baby vegetables.

FLASH-BAKED CHICKEN WITH LEMON

This dish was inspired by the simple but tasty Shaker style of cooking.

Preparation time: 3 minutes
Cooking time: 17 minutes
Makes 4 servings

1 tablespoon butter or margarine
1 tablespoon olive oil
1 pound boneless chicken breasts or thighs (skinned if desired)
1 tablespoon finely chopped fresh thyme *or* 1 teaspoon dried thyme
½ teaspoon salt
½ teaspoon freshly ground black pepper
2 tablespoons fresh lemon juice
4 thin slices lemon (optional)

Heat oven to 450°F. Place butter and oil in an ovenproof casserole dish. Place in oven to melt butter. Pound chicken to ½-inch thickness. Sprinkle with thyme, salt, and pepper. Place chicken in casserole and coat with butter mixture. Turn chicken skin-side up and sprinkle with lemon juice. Bake 15 to 17 minutes or until chicken is cooked through. Transfer chicken to a serving platter and pour juices from dish over chicken. Garnish with lemon slices, if desired.

Serving suggestions: Serve with hash brown potatoes and steamed mixed vegetables.

CHICKEN WITH CRANBERRY-WALNUT SAUCE

New England is famous for its cranberry bogs that produce most of the country's supply of the tart fruit. Thanks to canned cranberry sauce, this elegant dish can be made in minutes.

Preparation time: 5 minutes
Cooking time: 10 minutes
Makes 4 servings

2 whole chicken breasts, split and boned (skinned if desired)
1½ tablespoons Dijon-style mustard
1 tablespoon Grand Marnier or other orange-flavored liqueur
¼ cup canned whole cranberry sauce
1½ ounces cream cheese, softened
2 tablespoons coarsely chopped toasted walnuts

Pound chicken to ½-inch thickness. Combine mustard and liqueur; spread evenly over chicken. Broil chicken 4 to 5 inches from heat source until cooked through, about 5 minutes per side. Meanwhile, combine cranberry sauce and cream cheese, mixing until smooth. Stir in walnuts; serve alongside chicken.

Serving suggestions: Serve with steamed, sliced butternut or acorn squash and a tossed green salad.

DEVILED CHICKEN THIGHS

This four-ingredient recipe is sure to please dark meat chicken lovers. My children are particularly fond of the drumsticks. When substituting boneless chicken breasts, cut the cooking time from 16 to 10 minutes.

Preparation time: 4 minutes
Cooking time: 16 minutes
Makes 4 servings

2 tablespoons spicy brown or coarse-grained Dijon-style mustard
1 tablespoon olive oil
¼–½ teaspoon hot pepper sauce, as desired
4 large chicken thighs, boned, *or* 8 medium drumsticks

Combine mustard, oil, and pepper sauce. Spread evenly over all sides of chicken. Grill or broil 6 inches from heat source, turning once, until chicken is cooked through, about 16 minutes.

Serving suggestions: Serve with garlic pita or bagel chips and steamed or microwaved artichokes with a lemon-mayonnaise dipping sauce.

CHICKEN AND SAUSAGE STEW

This hearty dish typifies the midwest's large Polish community. Kielbasa, a Polish sausage, has more garlic than regular smoked sausage.

Preparation time: 5 minutes
Cooking time: 15 minutes
Makes 4 servings

½ pound fully cooked smoked sausage or kielbasa
½ pound boneless, skinless chicken breasts or thighs
½ teaspoon crushed dried thyme leaves
½ teaspoon freshly ground black pepper
1 14- to 16-ounce can whole tomatoes, drained
1 16-ounce can great northern beans, rinsed and drained
1 cup frozen corn kernels *or* 1 8-ounce can whole kernel corn, drained
½ cup beer, regular, light, or nonalcoholic
¼ teaspoon salt

Cut sausage into ½-inch slices. Place in a large skillet and cook over medium heat for 2 minutes. Meanwhile, cut chicken into 1-inch pieces; add to skillet. Sprinkle with thyme and pepper and cook, stirring constantly, for 2 minutes. Add remaining ingredients and bring to a boil. Simmer uncovered for 10 to 12 minutes or until chicken is cooked through and stew has thickened.

Serving suggestions: Serve with whole-grain rolls and a marinated cucumber salad.

THREE-PEPPER CHICKEN

This midwestern-inspired dish can be prepared quickly, using ingredients that are probably always on hand in your kitchen.

Preparation time: 5 minutes
Cooking time: 10 minutes
Makes 4 servings

2 whole chicken breasts, split and boned (skinned if desired)
1 tablespoon sweet Hungarian paprika
½ teaspoon coarsely ground black pepper
½ teaspoon cayenne pepper *or* hot Hungarian paprika
½ teaspoon salt
2 tablespoons olive oil

Pound chicken to ½-inch thickness. Combine seasonings; sprinkle evenly over chicken. Heat oil in a large skillet over medium-high heat. Cook chicken 2 minutes per side. Reduce heat to medium, cover skillet, and cook until chicken is cooked through, about 5 minutes.

Serving suggestions: Serve with oven-roasted garlic potatoes and buttered baby peas.

LEMON, GARLIC, AND HERB CHICKEN

Fresh herbs are easy to grow and can be kept in pots for transporting inside during cold weather. A small amount of fresh mint leaves adds an interesting flavor to this easy-to-make dish.

Preparation time: 8 minutes
Cooking time: 10 minutes
Makes 4 servings

¼ cup minced fresh herbs such as rosemary, tarragon, thyme, basil, chives, and oregano
2 tablespoons olive oil
Coarsely shredded peel from one lemon (1–1½ teaspoons)
2 cloves garlic, minced
2 whole chicken breasts, split and boned (skinned if desired)
4 wedges lemon

Combine herbs, oil, lemon peel, and garlic; spread over both sides of chicken. Grill or broil 4 to 5 inches from heat source, turning once, until chicken is cooked through, about 5 minutes per side. Serve with lemon wedges.

Serving suggestions: Serve with quick-cooking brown rice simmered in broth and sweet or red onion slices brushed with olive oil, salt, and pepper and grilled or broiled alongside chicken.

3
ETHNIC DISHES

Ethnic dishes are enjoying a rise in popularity, and for good reason. They are intriguing, exotic, and now much easier to duplicate at home due to the wealth of prepared sauces and condiments available in supermarkets throughout the country. Because of chicken's versatility, it lends itself to virtually any cuisine.

CHICKEN VERA CRUZ

An authentic Mexican recipe, this dish uses ingredients not normally associated with its native land. Capers and olives give this sauce a piquant and intriguing flavor.

Preparation time: 5 minutes
Cooking time: 12 minutes
Makes 4 servings

2 whole chicken breasts, split and boned (skinned if desired)
1 teaspoon ground coriander
½ teaspoon salt
¼–½ teaspoon cayenne pepper, as desired
1 tablespoon olive oil
1 8-ounce can stewed tomatoes
¼ cup pitted green olives
2 tablespoons drained capers
¼ cup coarsely chopped cilantro (optional)
4 wedges lime

Pound chicken to ½-inch thickness; sprinkle with coriander, salt, and cayenne pepper. Heat oil in a large skillet. Add chicken and cook over medium-high heat, 2 minutes per side. Add tomatoes, olives, and capers; simmer uncovered until chicken is cooked through and sauce has thickened, 6 to 8 minutes. Sprinkle with cilantro, if desired; serve with lime wedges.

Serving suggestions: Serve with brown or basmati rice and casaba or muskmelon slices.

CHICKEN ASADA

This Mexican dish is traditionally prepared with skirt steak but is every bit as flavorful with chicken.

Preparation time: 7 minutes
Cooking time: 12 minutes
Makes 4 servings

2 whole chicken breasts, split and boned (skinned, if desired)
1–2 tablespoons jalapeño relish *or* chopped canned jalapeño peppers, as desired
1 tablespoon vegetable oil
2 teaspoons ground cumin
½ teaspoon dried oregano
½ teaspoon salt
1 large clove garlic, minced
1 cup (4 ounces) shredded sharp cheddar cheese
¼ cup coarsely chopped cilantro (optional)

Preheat oven to 450°F. Pound chicken to ½-inch thickness. Combine jalapeño relish, oil, cumin, oregano, salt, and garlic, mixing well. Place chicken in a shallow baking dish large enough to hold chicken in one layer. Spread jalapeño relish mixture evenly over both sides of chicken. Turn chicken skin-side up and bake 10 minutes. Sprinkle with cheese and continue baking until chicken is cooked through and cheese has melted, about 2 minutes. Sprinkle with cilantro, if desired.

Serving suggestions: Serve with pinto beans and warm corn or flour tortillas.

PICADILLO CHICKEN

Picadillo (pronounced pee-kah-DEE-yo) is a traditional Mexican meat-and-vegetable hash. Here, the hash is rolled in flour tortillas and eaten like a burrito and it also makes a wonderful filling for stuffed peppers or enchiladas.

Preparation time: 8 minutes
Cooking time: 12 minutes
Makes 4 servings

1 pound boneless, skinless chicken breasts or chicken
   tenders
1 teaspoon ground cumin
¼ teaspoon ground cinnamon
¼ teaspoon salt
1 tablespoon vegetable oil
1 large yellow onion, coarsely chopped
2 cloves garlic, minced
1 8-ounce can stewed tomatoes
⅓ cup dark or golden raisins
¼ cup hot salsa *or* 2 tablespoons jalapeño relish
⅓ cup toasted slivered almonds
8 6- to 7-inch flour or corn tortillas, warmed
1 cup (4 ounces) shredded cheddar or Monterey Jack
   cheese

Cut chicken into ½-inch pieces and sprinkle with cumin, cinnamon, and salt. Heat oil in a large skillet over medium-high heat. Add chicken, onion, and garlic and cook, stirring frequently, until chicken is no longer pink, about 3 minutes. Add tomatoes, raisins, and salsa. Reduce heat to medium and simmer uncovered until sauce has thickened and chicken is cooked through, about 8 minutes. Stir in almonds and spoon into tortillas. Sprinkle with cheese. Fold tortilla over one end of filling and roll up.

Serving suggestions: Serve with cucumber and jicama sticks and Mexican beer.

CHICKEN FAJITAS

This traditional Mexican dish provides a sizzling pairing of flavors and textures. The marinade doubles as a salsa topping.

Preparation and standing time: 10 minutes
Cooking time: 10 minutes
Makes 4 servings

2 whole chicken breasts, split, boned, and skinned
1 teaspoon ground cumin
1 teaspoon garlic salt
¾ cup prepared salsa or picante sauce
¼ cup tequila
1 tablespoon olive oil
1 tablespoon fresh lime juice
8 6- to 7-inch flour tortillas, warmed

Optional Toppings
½ cup prepared guacamole or diced ripe avocado
1 small tomato, chopped (about ¾ cup)
½ cup coarsely chopped cilantro
½ cup regular or light sour cream

Sprinkle both sides of chicken with cumin and garlic salt and place in a shallow glass dish. Pour salsa, tequila, oil, and lime juice over chicken; turn to coat. Let stand 5 minutes. Remove chicken from marinade; reserve marinade. Grill or broil chicken 4 to 5 inches from heat source, 5 minutes per side or until chicken is cooked through, basting once on each side with marinade. Bring remaining marinade to a boil. Slice chicken crosswise into thin strips; serve in tortillas with toppings as desired. Drizzle with heated marinade.

Serving suggestions: Brush whole green onions with oil and grill or broil along with chicken. Serve as a side dish or add to the fajitas. A melon-ball salad makes a colorful and cooling accompaniment to the fajitas.

CHICKEN MOLE

Mole (pronounced MO-lay) is a unique Mexican sauce of unsweetened chocolate and hot peppers. Using prepared mole sauce saves an hour of preparation time and delivers long-cooked flavor. It may be found in the ethnic section of supermarkets or in Hispanic markets.

Preparation time: 3 minutes
Cooking time: 14 minutes
Makes 4 servings

1 pound boneless, skinless chicken thighs or breasts, or
  a combination of both
½ teaspoon salt
1 tablespoon olive oil
½ cup chicken broth
¼ cup prepared mole sauce
2 teaspoons toasted sesame seeds (optional)

Sprinkle chicken with salt. Heat oil in a large skillet. Add chicken and cook over medium-high heat, 2 minutes per side. Combine broth and mole sauce; pour over chicken. Cover and simmer until chicken is cooked through, 8 to 10 minutes. Sprinkle with sesame seeds, if desired.

Serving suggestions: Serve with short-grain, basmati, or other aromatic rice cooked in chicken broth with turmeric or powdered saffron, for an updated, flavorful, and colorful Mexican "yellow rice." Thawed frozen diced carrots and peas added to the rice at the end of the cooking time completes the meal.

HUNAN GRILLED CHICKEN

Centuries ago the province of Hunan refined the technique of grilling meats and serving them in spicy aromatic sauces. This fragrant dish will please the palates of spicy food lovers. Hot pepper oil and hoisin sauce are available in the ethnic section of large supermarkets or Oriental markets.

Preparation time: 5 minutes
Cooking time: 10 minutes
Makes 4 servings

2 tablespoons prepared hoisin sauce
2 teaspoons soy sauce
1 clove garlic, minced
1 teaspoon hot pepper oil
2 whole chicken breasts, split and boned (skinned, if
  desired)

Combine hoisin sauce, soy sauce, garlic, and oil; mix well. Spread over both sides of chicken. Grill or broil chicken 4 to 5 inches from heat source until chicken is cooked through, about 5 minutes per side.

Serving suggestions: Serve with a cantaloupe and blueberry salad and vegetable fried rice.

SZECHUAN STIR-FRY

Szechuan-style cooking has existed for 5,000 years but only reached the States in the early 1970s. Szechuan peppercorns have become a primary ingredient in Chinese cooking. Less exotic than they sound, they add a spicy-sweet note to this dish. They are found in the ethnic food section of most large supermarkets.

Preparation time: 12 minutes
Cooking time: 8 minutes
Makes 4 servings

1 pound chicken tenders or boneless, skinless chicken
   breasts, cut into 1-inch pieces
2 tablespoons soy sauce
2 cloves garlic, minced
1 tablespoon finely shredded fresh ginger
1 teaspoon crushed Szechuan peppercorns *or* ½
   teaspoon red pepper flakes
2 tablespoons peanut or vegetable oil
1 small red bell pepper, cut into ½-inch pieces
2 tablespoons water
2 teaspoons cornstarch
4 green onions, cut diagonally into 1-inch pieces
¼ cup coarsely chopped peanuts (optional)
¼ cup coarsely chopped cilantro (optional)

Combine chicken, soy sauce, garlic, ginger, and pepper-corns in a medium-sized bowl; set aside. Heat oil in a wok or large skillet over medium-high heat. When oil is hot, add chicken mixture. Stir-fry just until chicken is no longer pink. Add red pepper and stir-fry for 3 minutes. In a small bowl, combine water and cornstarch and stir into chicken mixture. Add onions and stir-fry for 1 minute or until sauce has thickened. Sprinkle with peanuts and cilantro, if desired.

Serving suggestions: Serve with cooked ramen noodles or white rice and nappa cabbage slaw.

CASHEW CHICKEN

There is no richer nut flavor than cashew. Blending its texture and taste with chicken enhances the richness of both. Complete the dinner with a package of fortune cookies, available in the Oriental section of the supermarket where you will also find the hoisin sauce and sesame oil.

Preparation time: 12 minutes
Cooking time: 6 minutes
Makes 4 servings

2 tablespoons prepared hoisin or plum sauce
1 tablespoon soy sauce
1 tablespoon water
2 teaspoons cornstarch
1 teaspoon Oriental sesame oil
2 tablespoons peanut or vegetable oil
1 pound chicken tenders or boneless, skinless chicken
    breasts, cut into 1-inch pieces
3–4 ounces fresh shiitake mushrooms, stems discarded,
    caps sliced
2 cloves garlic, minced
¼–½ teaspoon red pepper flakes, as desired
3 green onions, cut diagonally into ½-inch pieces
¼ cup coarsely chopped cashews

Combine hoisin sauce, soy sauce, water, cornstarch, and sesame oil; set aside. Heat peanut oil in a large wok or skillet over medium-high heat. When oil is hot, add chicken, mushrooms, garlic, and pepper flakes. Stir-fry until chicken is no longer pink, 2 to 3 minutes. Add sauce mixture and green onions. Stir-fry until sauce has thickened and chicken is cooked through, about 2 minutes. Stir in cashews.

Serving suggestions: Serve with egg rolls and fresh, ripe papaya wedges.

SESAME CHICKEN NUGGETS WITH SWEET-SOUR SAUCE

This recipe offers a unique combination of chicken, sesame, and the popular Chinese sweet-and-sour sauce. Serve these tender morsels in place of fat-soaked prepared chicken nuggets. They are great as an informal appetizer for your next dinner party.

Preparation time: 10 minutes
Cooking time: 6 minutes
Makes 4 servings, or about 2 dozen appetizers

Sweet-Sour Sauce (see Note)
2 tablespoons very hot water
½ teaspoon dry mustard
½ cup apricot preserves

Sesame Chicken Nuggets
1 egg white, beaten
2 teaspoons finely shredded fresh ginger
2 cloves garlic, minced
¾ teaspoon salt
1 pound chicken tenders or boneless, skinless chicken
    breasts, cut into 1-inch pieces
½ cup sesame seeds
¼ cup peanut or vegetable oil

To make the sweet-sour sauce, combine hot water and mustard in a small bowl. Add preserves; mix well and set aside. To prepare the sesame chicken nuggets, combine egg white, ginger, garlic, and salt in a shallow bowl or pie plate; mix well. Dip chicken pieces in egg mixture; shake off excess. Coat lightly with sesame seeds, pressing gently to slightly flatten chicken. Heat oil in a large skillet over medium-high heat. Add chicken and cook until golden brown and cooked through, about 3 minutes per side. Serve with sauce.

Note: For an even quicker dish, use prepared sweet-and-sour or plum sauce for dipping.

Serving suggestions: Serve with cooked udon or fettuccine noodles tossed with green onions, soy sauce, and sesame oil and steamed or microwaved Chinese vegetables.

HOT AND SOUR CHICKEN STEW

This flavorful stew gets its mild sour taste from rice wine vinegar, found in the ethnic section of the supermarket. Adjust the pepper flakes according to the heat level you prefer.

Preparation time: 10 minutes
Cooking time: 9 minutes
Makes 4 servings

1 pound chicken tenders or boneless, skinless chicken breasts, cut into 1-inch pieces
2 tablespoons light soy sauce
3–4 ounces fresh shiitake mushrooms
2 tablespoons peanut or vegetable oil
2 cloves garlic, minced
½–1 teaspoon red pepper flakes, as desired
1 14-ounce can chicken broth
2 tablespoons rice-wine vinegar
2 teaspoons Oriental sesame oil
1½ tablespoons cornstarch
3 tablespoons cold water
2 cups sliced bok choy or nappa cabbage
¼ cup thinly sliced green onion

Sprinkle chicken with soy sauce and set aside. Discard stems from mushrooms. Slice caps in half and set aside. Heat peanut oil in a large saucepan over medium-high heat. Add chicken mixture, garlic, and pepper flakes. Cook, stirring constantly, for 2 minutes. Add broth, vinegar, sesame oil, and reserved mushroom caps and bring to a boil. Simmer uncovered until chicken is cooked through, about

2 minutes. In a small bowl, combine cornstarch with water and stir into stew. Cook, stirring frequently, until sauce has thickened. Stir in bok choy and green onion; heat through.

Serving suggestions: Serve with chow mein noodles and fresh pineapple spears.

MU SHU CHICKEN

This popular Mandarin dish is easy to prepare at home. If your supermarket has a salad bar, buy the vegetables precut and save even more preparation time. Plum sauce and Mandarin pancakes may be found in Oriental markets or some large supermarkets.

Preparation time: 16 minutes
Cooking time: 4 minutes
Makes 4 servings

½ pound boneless, skinless chicken breasts or chicken tenders
¼ cup soy sauce
2 teaspoons cornstarch
1 tablespoon peanut or vegetable oil
2 cloves garlic, minced
½ teaspoon red pepper flakes
2 cups shredded green cabbage
2 cups fresh bean sprouts
2 medium carrots, shredded (about ½ cup)
½ cup sliced green onions with tops
½ cup plum sauce
8 purchased Mandarin pancakes or large lettuce leaves

Cut chicken into short, thin strips. Combine soy sauce and cornstarch, mixing well. Toss chicken with soy sauce mixture and set aside while preparing the vegetables. Heat oil in a wok or large skillet over medium-high heat. Add chicken mixture, garlic, and pepper flakes and stir-fry 1 minute. Add cabbage, bean sprouts, carrots, and onions and continue to stir-fry until chicken is cooked through and cabbage is tender, about 3 minutes. Spread about 1 table-spoon plum sauce onto each pancake or lettuce leaf. Divide chicken mixture evenly onto each pancake or let-tuce leaf and roll up. Serve with additional plum sauce, if desired.

Serving suggestions: Serve with steamed white rice and Chinese beer or green tea.

GRILLED TERIYAKI CHICKEN

A long-standing favorite at our house, this recipe is easy to double or cut in half as needed. Leftover chicken turns fried rice into a second main dish the following day.

Preparation and standing time: 10 minutes
Cooking time: 10 minutes
Makes 4 servings

2 whole chicken breasts, split and boned (skinned, if
   desired)
¼ cup light soy sauce
¼ cup dry sherry
2 cloves garlic, minced
½ teaspoon red pepper flakes

Place chicken in a shallow glass dish. Combine remaining ingredients; pour over chicken. Let stand 5 minutes, turning once. Grill or broil chicken 4 to 5 inches from heat source, basting once with marinade, until chicken is cooked through, about 5 minutes per side. Bring remaining marinade to a boil to serve as a dipping sauce for chicken.

Serving suggestions: Serve with white rice and stir-fried Oriental vegetables.

SPICY SATAY STRIPS

This appetizer is a favorite at our annual holiday party.

Preparation time: 13 minutes
Cooking time: 7 minutes
Makes 4 servings, or 8–10 appetizers

1 pound skinless, boneless chicken breasts or chicken
  tenders
¼ cup soy sauce
¼ cup rice wine (sake) or dry sherry
2 tablespoons peanut or vegetable oil
3 cloves garlic, minced
1 tablespoon brown sugar
½ teaspoon red pepper flakes

Cut chicken lengthwise into ½-inch strips and place in a shallow glass dish. Combine remaining ingredients and pour over chicken, turning to coat. Thread chicken onto metal skewers or bamboo skewers that have been soaked in hot water; reserve marinade. Place skewers over ash-covered coals or on the rack of a broiler pan; baste with half of reserved marinade. Grill or broil 4 to 5 inches from heat source for 4 minutes. Turn and baste with remaining marinade. Continue grilling or broiling until chicken is cooked through, about 3 minutes.

Serving suggestions: Serve with pickled ginger and stir-fried pea pods and red pepper strips with a small amount of orange marmalade stirred in at the end.

GINGERED CHICKEN

The cooks of Indonesia and Malaysia have a flair for combining many divergent spices, as this delicious recipe illustrates. For a spicier dish, add ¼ teaspoon red pepper flakes to the soy sauce mixture.

Preparation time: 8 minutes
Cooking time: 12 minutes
Makes 4 servings

2 whole chicken breasts, split and boned (skinned if desired)
1 teaspoon ground cumin
1 teaspoon ground coriander
1 tablespoon vegetable or olive oil
¼ cup light soy sauce
2 tablespoons water
1 tablespoon fresh lemon juice
1 tablespoon finely shredded fresh ginger
2 cloves garlic, minced
⅓ cup coarsely chopped cilantro (optional)

Sprinkle chicken evenly with cumin and coriander. Heat oil in a large skillet. Add chicken and cook over medium-high heat, 2 minutes per side. Meanwhile, combine soy sauce, water, lemon juice, ginger, and garlic. Pour over chicken, reduce heat to medium, and continue cooking for 3 minutes. Turn chicken; continue cooking for 3 minutes or until chicken is cooked through and sauce has thickened. Transfer to a serving platter and spoon pan juices over chicken. Sprinkle with cilantro, if desired.

Serving suggestions: Serve with egg noodles and steamed or microwaved zucchini and yellow squash.

COCONUT CHICKEN

███▬███▬███▬███▬███▬███▬███▬███▬███▬██

This traditional Thai dish (Kai P'anaeng) has a subtle but exotic sauce of unsweetened coconut milk. Canned coconut milk is available in Oriental markets and some large supermarkets.

Preparation time: 4 minutes
Cooking time: 12 minutes
Makes 4 servings

2 whole chicken breasts, split and boned (skinned, if desired)
1 tablespoon peanut or vegetable oil
3 cloves garlic, minced
1 teaspoon ground coriander
½ teaspoon red pepper flakes
½ cup canned coconut milk
1 tablespoon soy sauce
½ teaspoon finely shredded lemon peel
2 tablespoons minced green onion

Pound chicken to ½-inch thickness. Heat oil in a large skillet over medium heat. Add chicken and garlic. Sprinkle chicken with coriander and pepper flakes. Cook until lightly browned, about 2 minutes per side. Add coconut milk and soy sauce. Simmer uncovered until chicken is cooked through and sauce has thickened, about 8 minutes. Stir in lemon peel and sprinkle with onion.

Serving suggestions: Serve with a mixed vegetable salad and brown rice.

THAI CHICKEN AND NOODLES

Perhaps the most striking of Oriental dishes, this Thai original is intense in both texture and taste. It is the peanut butter that gives the sauce a velvety texture and authentic Thai flavor.

Preparation time: 15 minutes
Cooking time: 5 minutes
Makes 4 servings

6 ounces udon noodles or vermicelli, broken in half
1 pound boneless, skinless chicken breasts or chicken tenders
2 cloves garlic, minced
½ teaspoon red pepper flakes
2 tablespoons peanut or vegetable oil
¼ cup chicken broth
2 tablespoons creamy peanut butter
2 tablespoons soy sauce
3 green onions, cut diagonally into ½-inch pieces
1 teaspoon Oriental sesame oil

Cook noodles according to package directions; drain. While noodles are cooking, cut chicken into 1-inch pieces and toss with garlic and pepper flakes. Heat oil in a large skillet over medium-high heat. Add chicken mixture and stir-fry until chicken is cooked through, about 3 minutes. Add broth, peanut butter, and soy sauce. Cook, stirring constantly, until peanut butter has melted and sauce has thickened. Add green onions, sesame oil, and drained noodles; cook and stir until heated through and noodles are coated with sauce (about 1 minute).

Serving suggestions: Serve with thinly sliced cucumbers and onions (marinated in rice wine vinegar and a pinch of sugar) and steamed sugar snap peas.

MIEN GA
(VIETNAMESE CHICKEN SOUP)

This quick chicken soup boasts the fabulous flavors of Vietnamese cooking. Cellophane noodles, sometimes called bean threads, and fish sauce are found in Oriental or specialty foods markets.

Preparation time: 5 minutes
Cooking time: 10 minutes
Makes 4 servings

1 ounce cellophane noodles
½ pound boneless, skinless chicken breasts, thighs, or
   chicken tenders
1 tablespoon peanut or vegetable oil
2 cloves garlic, minced
2 teaspoons finely shredded fresh ginger
¼ teaspoon red pepper flakes
2 14-ounce cans chicken broth
2 tablespoons fish sauce or soy sauce
2 tablespoons coarsely chopped cilantro
2 tablespoons thinly sliced green onion tops

Soak noodles in very hot tap water to cover. While noodles are soaking, cut chicken into short, thin strips. Heat oil in a large saucepan over medium-high heat. Add chicken, garlic, ginger, and pepper flakes. Cook, stirring constantly, 1 minute. Add broth and fish sauce; bring to a boil. Reduce heat to medium and simmer uncovered until chicken is cooked through, about 8 minutes. Drain noodles and cut into 1-inch pieces. Arrange in bottoms of four soup bowls. Ladle soup over noodles and sprinkle with cilantro and green onion tops.

Serving suggestions: Serve with slices of ripe papaya or mango and steamed rice seasoned with soy sauce.

CHUTNEY-MUSTARD GLAZED CHICKEN

The sweet-hot flavor of chutney and spicy mustard will mellow deliciously upon cooking. For a more intensely flavored dish, mix up additional chutney and mustard to use as a dipping sauce for the cooked chicken.

Preparation time: 5 minutes
Cooking time: 10 minutes
Makes 4 servings

2 whole chicken breasts, split, boned, and skinned
⅓ cup chopped mango chutney
1 tablespoon spicy brown or coarse-grained mustard

Pound chicken to ½-inch thickness and place on the rack of a broiler pan. Combine chutney and mustard; brush half of mixture evenly over chicken. Broil 4 to 5 inches from heat source for 5 minutes. Turn; brush remaining chutney mixture evenly over chicken. Broil for 5 minutes or until chicken is cooked through and glaze is bubbly.

Serving suggestions: Serve with a red leaf lettuce salad dressed in creamy garlic dressing and boiled new potatoes with butter and parsley.

TANDOORI-STYLE CHICKEN

The yogurt acts as a tenderizing agent to produce succulent chicken in this quick version of a famous Indian dish.

Preparation time: 7 minutes
Cooking time: 10 minutes
Makes 4 servings

2 whole chicken breasts, split, boned, and skinned
½ cup plain yogurt
2 cloves garlic, minced
1 teaspoon ground coriander
1 teaspoon turmeric
½ teaspoon crushed saffron threads *or* ¼ teaspoon
   ground saffron
½ teaspoon salt
¼ teaspoon cayenne pepper
¼ cup coarsely chopped cilantro (optional)
4 wedges lime

Pound chicken to ½-inch thickness. Combine yogurt and seasonings and pour evenly over chicken, turning to coat. Grill or broil 4 to 5 inches from heat source until chicken is cooked through, about 5 minutes per side, basting once on each side with yogurt mixture. Sprinkle with cilantro, if desired. Serve with lime wedges.

Serving suggestions: Serve with couscous cooked in broth with currants and almonds and buttered baby peas.

CURRIED CHICKEN

Spicy-sweet flavors enhance the chicken in this flavorful dish. Yogurt is a traditional Indian topping that adds tartness while cooling the fire from the spices.

Preparation time: 7 minutes
Cooking time: 13 minutes
Makes 4 servings

2 tablespoons flour
1 teaspoon salt
¼ teaspoon cayenne pepper
1 pound chicken tenders or boneless, skinless chicken
  breasts, cut into 1½-inch pieces
2 tablespoons vegetable oil
1 tablespoon curry powder
1 medium yellow onion, cut into thin wedges
2 cloves garlic, minced
1 cup chicken broth
⅓ cup golden raisins
1½ tablespoons tomato paste
¼ cup coarsely chopped cilantro
¼ cup plain yogurt

Combine flour, salt, and cayenne pepper in a plastic bag. Add chicken in two batches; shake to coat. Heat oil in a large skillet over medium-high heat. Add chicken and cook until lightly browned on all sides, about 2 minutes. Add curry powder and toss to coat. Add onion and garlic and cook for 2 minutes. Add broth, raisins, and tomato paste and simmer uncovered for 8 minutes or until chicken is cooked through and sauce has thickened. Sprinkle with cilantro and garnish with a dollop of yogurt.

Serving suggestions: Serve with spinach noodles and slices of casaba or muskmelon.

MOROCCAN CHICKEN SAUTE

Moroccan cuisine employs the technique of artfully blending pungent spices into exotic and intriguing combinations. Tangines, or stews, are usually cooked for hours. This quick dish will give you the flavors of Morocco without the time-consuming method.

Preparation time: 7 minutes
Cooking time: 12 minutes
Makes 4 servings

1 teaspoon paprika
½ teaspoon ground cumin
½ teaspoon salt
¼ teaspoon powdered saffron or ground turmeric
⅛ teaspoon ground ginger
2 whole chicken breasts, split and boned (skinned if desired)
2 tablespoons butter or margarine
1 small yellow onion, finely chopped
2 cloves garlic, minced
½ cup chicken broth
¼ cup raisins
¼ cup slivered almonds, toasted
¼ cup coarsely chopped cilantro

Combine paprika, cumin, salt, saffron, and ginger, and sprinkle over chicken. Heat butter in a large skillet over medium-high heat. Add chicken, skin-side down, and cook for 2 minutes. Turn; add onion and garlic and continue to cook for 2 minutes. Reduce heat to medium. Add broth and raisins; simmer uncovered until chicken is cooked through, about 6 minutes, stirring occasionally. Transfer chicken to a serving platter; increase heat to high and cook sauce to desired consistency. Stir in almonds; pour over chicken. Sprinkle with cilantro.

Serving suggestions: Serve with bulgur (cracked wheat) pilaf and a steamed green vegetable.

JAMAICAN JERKED CHICKEN

Traditional jerked chicken is marinated several hours or overnight in chili peppers and seasonings before being grilled. Thanks to the pungent Pickapeppa sauce, widely available in the sauce section of the supermarket, this process may be eliminated and replaced by a much quicker grilling method.

Preparation time: 5 minutes
Cooking time: 11 minutes
Makes 4 servings

2 whole chicken breasts, split and boned (skinned, if desired)
1 teaspoon dried thyme
½ teaspoon salt
¼ teaspoon ground allspice
½ cup Pickapeppa sauce
1 teaspoon sugar
2 tablespoons minced green onion tops
4 wedges lime

Sprinkle chicken with thyme, salt, and allspice. Place over ash-covered coals or on the rack of a broiler pan. Combine Pickapeppa sauce and sugar. Brush half of Pickapeppa sauce mixture over chicken. Grill or broil 4 to 5 inches from heat source for 4 to 5 minutes. Turn and brush remaining Pickapeppa sauce mixture over chicken. Continue to grill or broil until chicken is cooked through, 5 to 6 minutes. Sprinkle with green onions and serve with lime wedges.

Serving suggestions: Serve with red beans and white rice.

4
CONTINENTAL DISHES

The European culinary tradition is unmatched. Its contributions and standards of excellence continue to influence the history of food, both past and present. In this section you'll find classic recipes from the continent, updated and streamlined for minimum preparation and maximum enjoyment.

MYKONOS CHICKEN SALAD

This salad was inspired by a trip to the Greek Islands, where the food is always fresh and delicious. It's perfect for warm summer nights or whenever a light entree is in order.

Preparation time: 8 minutes
Cooking time: 12 minutes
Makes 4 servings

2 whole chicken breasts, split, boned, and skinned
3 tablespoons olive oil
2 cloves garlic, minced
1 teaspoon dried oregano, crushed
½ teaspoon dried thyme
½ teaspoon salt
½ teaspoon freshly ground black pepper
4 cups sliced romaine lettuce
1 large tomato, cut into 8 wedges
½ small cucumber, sliced
12 Kalamata olives (optional)
2 tablespoons red wine vinegar or lemon juice
½ cup (2 ounces) crumbled feta cheese

Pound chicken into ½-inch thickness. Heat oil in a large skillet over medium heat. Add chicken and garlic; sprinkle with oregano, thyme, salt, and pepper. Cook for 4 to 5 minutes per side or until chicken is cooked through. While chicken is cooking, arrange lettuce on a serving platter. Arrange tomato, cucumber, and olives around edges of lettuce. Transfer chicken to a carving board and slice crosswise into ½-inch strips. Place chicken over lettuce. Add vinegar or lemon juice to remaining oil in skillet and mix well. Pour over chicken and lettuce; sprinkle with cheese.

Serving suggestions: Serve with heated Syrian flat bread (like pita without the pocket) and steamed or roasted new potatoes with rosemary, garlic, and Parmesan cheese.

GRILLED CHICKEN WITH OLIVE-ANCHOVY BUTTER

The French are exceptionally fond of seasoned butters and use them profusely on simply grilled meats and vegetables. Niçoise olives may be found in large supermarkets or specialty stores. Pitted ripe olives may be substituted but will not be as flavorful.

Preparation time: 5 minutes
Cooking time: 10 minutes
Makes 4 servings

2 whole chicken breasts, split and boned (skinned if desired)
1 tablespoon olive oil
Salt and freshly ground black pepper to taste
⅓ cup Niçoise olives (see Note)
¼ cup butter or margarine, softened
2–3 anchovy fillets, mashed, or 1 tablespoon anchovy paste

Brush chicken lightly with oil and sprinkle with salt and pepper. Grill or broil chicken 4 to 5 inches from heat source until cooked through, about 5 minutes per side. Meanwhile, seed and chop olives. Combine butter, olives, and anchovies until well mixed. Divide butter over hot chicken just before serving.

Note: Three tablespoons of prepared imported olive spread, available in large supermarkets and specialty stores, may be substituted for the olives.

Serving suggestions: Serve with a vinaigrette romaine salad with sun-dried tomatoes and goat cheese and crusty French hard rolls.

RASPBERRY-SHALLOT CHICKEN SUPREMES

The French aptly named boneless chicken breasts "suprêmes," meaning the best of the chicken. To make fresh raspberry vinegar, pour 2 cups of white wine vinegar over 1 pint of berries. Let stand, covered, in a clean glass jar at room temperature for two weeks. Strain and discard the raspberries and store the vinegar tightly covered in a cool, dark place for up to one year.

Preparation time: 5 minutes
Cooking time: 14 minutes
Makes 4 servings

2 whole chicken breasts, split, boned, and skinned
½ teaspoon salt
2 tablespoons butter or margarine
2 large shallots, sliced, *or* ¼ cup diced sweet onion
¼ cup (raspberry) vinegar (homemade or purchased) orange j
½ cup chicken broth
¼ cup whipping cream
1 tablespoon tomato paste

Pound chicken to ½-inch thickness and sprinkle with salt. Heat butter in a large skillet. Add shallots and cook over medium-high heat for 1 minute. Push shallots to the edge of the skillet. Add chicken and brown lightly, about 2 minutes per side. Using a slotted spatula, transfer chicken to a plate. Increase heat to high and add vinegar to skillet. Cook and stir until sauce is reduced to a syrupy glaze, about 1 minute. Add broth, cream, and tomato paste and reduce heat to medium. Stir well and return chicken to skillet. Cover and simmer for 5 minutes or until chicken is cooked through. Transfer chicken to a serving platter and increase heat to high. Cook sauce to desired consistency and pour over chicken.

Serving suggestions: Serve with pasta (tomato fettuccine is especially delicious with this dish) and steamed asparagus or broccoli.

CHICKEN PROVENCAL

Away from the Normandy coast, poultry and game are served often in the villages of Provence. Leeks and garlic are staples common to almost all dishes, and the abundant fresh ingredients of the region, including savory herbs, tomatoes, and peppers, make for thoroughly flavorful meals.

Preparation time: 6 minutes
Cooking time: 14 minutes
Makes 4 servings

6 ounces uncooked capellini or very thin spaghetti
2 whole chicken breasts, split, boned, and skinned
Salt and freshly ground black pepper to taste
2 tablespoons olive oil
3 cloves garlic, minced
1 16-ounce can tomatoes, undrained
1 large leek
1 7-ounce jar roasted red bell peppers
3 tablespoons tomato paste
1 tablespoon minced fresh thyme leaves *or* 1 teaspoon
    dried thyme

Cook capellini according to package directions; drain and keep warm on a serving platter. While capellini is cooking, sprinkle chicken with salt and pepper to taste. Heat oil in a large skillet. Add chicken and garlic and cook over medium-high heat for 2 minutes. Reduce heat to medium. Turn chicken over and add tomatoes. Thinly slice the white portion of leek and add to skillet. Drain and coarsely chop red peppers and add to skillet. Stir in tomato paste and thyme. Cover and simmer until chicken is cooked through, about 8 minutes. Place chicken on capellini. Cook and stir sauce for 1 minute. Pour over chicken and capellini.

Serving suggestions: Serve with toasted garlic bread and prepared imported olive spread (minced Niçoise olives, found in large supermarkets or specialty markets) or whole Niçoise olives.

BAKED CHICKEN MILANAISE

In France, this simple dish is often sautéed in lots of clarified butter. This version bakes unwatched while attention is directed to the rest of the meal.

Preparation time: 8 minutes
Cooking time: 12 minutes
Makes 4 servings

2 whole chicken breasts, split, boned, and skinned
3 tablespoons butter or margarine, melted
¼ teaspoon salt
¼ teaspoon freshly ground black pepper
½ cup fresh bread crumbs (see Note)
½ cup grated Parmesan cheese

Optional Dipping Sauce
2 tablespoons tarragon or regular Dijon-style mustard
2 tablespoons light mayonnaise

Preheat oven to 450°F. Pound chicken to ½-inch thickness. Combine butter, salt, and pepper in a shallow dish. Combine bread crumbs and cheese in another shallow dish. Dip chicken in butter mixture, then roll in bread-crumb mixture and pat to coat. Place on a foil-lined baking sheet and bake until chicken is golden brown and cooked through, about 12 minutes. If desired, combine mustard and mayonnaise for a dipping sauce to serve with chicken.

Note: To make fresh bread crumbs, process torn sliced bread in food processor or blender.

Serving suggestions: Serve with broiled tomato halves and drained canned white asparagus spears with a vinaigrette dressing.

CHICKEN VERONIQUE

This classic French dish is often prepared with fish but is even more flavorful with chicken.

Preparation time: 3 minutes
Cooking time: 17 minutes
Makes 4 servings

1 tablespoon flour
¾ teaspoon salt, divided
¼ teaspoon ground white pepper
2 whole chicken breasts, split and boned (skinned, if desired)
2 tablespoons butter or margarine
½ cup dry white wine or vermouth
1 cup seedless green grapes
½ cup heavy cream
½ teaspoon dried chervil
2 tablespoons chopped fresh chives (optional)

Combine flour, ½ teaspoon of the salt, and pepper in a bag. Add chicken and shake to coat well. Heat butter in a skillet over medium-high heat. Add chicken and cook until lightly browned, about 2 minutes per side. Add wine and grapes to skillet. Reduce heat to medium; cover and simmer until chicken is cooked through, 5 to 6 minutes. Transfer chicken and grapes to a serving platter. Increase heat to high and boil juices until reduced to about ½ cup. Add cream, chervil, and remaining salt. Continue to boil until sauce has thickened, about 3 minutes. Pour over chicken and grapes and sprinkle with chives.

Serving suggestions: Serve with oven-roasted vegetables and crusty French bread.

QUICK COQ AU VIN

Red wine gives this sauce its especially rich flavor. Beaujolais is a particularly good choice for this dish.

Preparation time: 10 minutes
Cooking time: 10 minutes
Makes 4 servings

3 tablespoons flour
1 teaspoon salt
½ teaspoon freshly ground black pepper
1 pound skinless, boneless chicken breasts or thighs, or
  a combination of both
2 tablespoons olive oil or butter
1 large yellow onion, coarsely chopped
4 ounces white mushrooms, halved (or quartered if large)
2 cloves garlic, minced
⅓ cup chicken broth
¼ cup dry red wine

Combine flour, salt, and pepper and dredge chicken in the flour mixture. Heat oil in a large skillet over medium-high heat. Add chicken, onion, mushrooms, and garlic. Cook chicken 2 minutes per side, stirring vegetables once. Add broth and wine and reduce heat to medium. Simmer uncovered until chicken is cooked through, about 6 minutes. Transfer chicken to a serving platter, leaving vegetables and sauce in skillet. Increase heat to high and cook until sauce is desired consistency. Pour over chicken.

Serving suggestions: Serve with cooked orzo (rice-shaped pasta) and a mixed berry salad.

PRIMAVERA CHICKEN AND PASTA

This colorful pasta dish celebrates the arrival of early spring vegetables. A few extra minutes of preparation are needed to shell fresh peas, but the flavor and texture are well worth the effort.

Preparation time: 12 minutes
Cooking time: 8 minutes
Makes 4 servings

6 ounces uncooked penne, ziti, shell, or rotini pasta
¾ pound chicken tenders or boneless, skinless chicken breasts, cut into 1-inch pieces
½ teaspoon salt
¼ teaspoon freshly ground black pepper
2 tablespoons olive oil
1 large sweet onion, cut into ½-inch pieces
1 medium red bell pepper, cut into ½-inch pieces
1 cup 1-inch asparagus pieces
½ cup frozen baby peas or shelled fresh peas
2 cloves garlic, minced
½ cup whipping cream or half-and-half
¼ cup coarsely chopped fresh basil *or* mixed fresh herbs such as thyme, dill, tarragon, chives, or Italian parsley
¼ cup grated Parmesan cheese
Freshly ground black pepper to taste

Cook pasta according to package directions. While pasta is cooking, sprinkle chicken with salt and pepper. Heat oil in a 12-inch skillet over medium-high heat. Add chicken and cook for 3 minutes or until chicken is no longer pink, stirring occasionally. Remove chicken and set aside. Add vegetables and garlic to skillet. Reduce heat, cover, and cook for 3 minutes. Uncover and add chicken and cream. Cook and stir for 1 minute. Stir in drained pasta and heat through. Stir in basil. Remove the skillet from heat and toss in cheese. Serve with pepper.

Serving suggestions: Serve with sourdough bread sticks and a bibb lettuce salad with balsamic vinaigrette and bacon bits.

CHICKEN PICATTA

This version of a popular Northern Italian dish is just as satisfying and less expensive than the traditional veal recipe.

Preparation time: 5 minutes
Cooking time: 12 minutes
Makes 4 servings

2 whole chicken breasts, split and boned (skinned if desired)
¼ cup flour
½ teaspoon salt
¼ teaspoon freshly ground black pepper
2 tablespoons butter
2 tablespoons olive oil
2 cloves garlic, minced
¼ cup dry white wine or vermouth
2 tablespoons fresh lemon juice
3 tablespoons drained capers
¼ cup minced fresh parsley, preferably Italian
4 thin slices lemon (optional)

Pound chicken to ½-inch thickness. Combine flour, salt, and pepper and dredge chicken in flour mixture. Heat butter, oil, and garlic in a large skillet over medium heat. Add chicken and cook until golden brown and cooked through, about 4 minutes per side. Transfer to a serving platter; keep warm. Add wine and lemon juice to skillet; cook and stir until sauce is desired consistency. Stir in capers and pour sauce over chicken. Sprinkle with parsley and garnish with lemon slices, if desired.

Serving suggestions: Serve with angel hair pasta and steamed asparagus spears sprinkled with Parmesan.

CHICKEN WITH PROSCIUTTO AND PROVOLONE

This easy dish flaunts the fabulous flavor of prosciutto, an Italian cured ham, and provolone cheese found in Italian grocery stores or large supermarket deli departments. If these are unavailable, substitute smoked ham and mozzarella cheese.

Preparation time: 5 minutes
Cooking time: 10 minutes
Makes 4 servings

2 whole chicken breasts, split, boned, and skinned
½ teaspoon freshly ground black pepper
1 tablespoon olive oil
2 cloves garlic, halved
4 thin slices prosciutto
4 thin slices provolone cheese

Pound chicken to ½-inch thickness; sprinkle evenly with pepper. Heat oil and garlic in a large skillet over medium heat. Add chicken and cook for 4 minutes; turn and cook for 2 more minutes. Lay prosciutto and cheese over chicken. Continue cooking until chicken is cooked through and cheese is melted, about 3 minutes.

Serving suggestions: Serve with sautéed mushrooms with a splash of balsamic vinegar and a fresh fruit compote.

CHICKEN PUTTANESCA

Puttanesca refers to an Italian quick tomato sauce usually served over capellini as a side dish. The addition of chicken makes this quick and easy recipe a hearty main dish.

Preparation time: 5 minutes
Cooking time: 12 minutes
Makes 4 servings

8 ounces uncooked capellini or very thin spaghetti
1 pound boneless chicken breasts or chicken tenders
2 tablespoons olive oil
3 cloves garlic, chopped or sliced
½ teaspoon red pepper flakes
1 16-ounce can plum tomatoes, undrained
1 2¼-ounce can sliced ripe olives, drained
2 tablespoons tomato paste
1 tablespoon drained capers
1 tablespoon anchovy paste (optional)
¼ cup chopped fresh Italian or regular parsley (optional)
¼ cup (1 ounce) grated Parmesan cheese

Cook capellini according to package directions. Drain and keep warm on a serving platter. While capellini is cooking, cut chicken into ½-inch pieces. Heat oil in a large skillet over medium-high heat. Add chicken, garlic, and pepper flakes. Cook, stirring constantly, until chicken is no longer pink, about 2 minutes. Add tomatoes, breaking up with a wooden spoon. Stir in olives, tomato paste, capers, and, if desired, anchovy paste. Simmer uncovered until sauce has thickened and chicken is cooked through, about 6 minutes. Stir in parsley, if desired. Spoon over capellini and sprinkle with cheese.

Serving suggestions: Serve with soft Italian bread sticks and an antipasto salad.

CHICKEN PARMIGIANA

One of the most popular flavor combinations of Southern Italy is found in this version of parmigiana. Aged Parmesano-Reggiano cheese may be found in specialty grocery stores or large supermarkets and delis.

Preparation time: 8 minutes
Cooking time: 10 minutes
Makes 4 servings

2 whole chicken breasts, split, boned, and skinned *cut up*
3 tablespoons flour
½ teaspoon salt
¼ teaspoon freshly ground black pepper
2 tablespoons olive oil
2 cloves garlic, coarsely chopped
1 cup prepared spaghetti sauce
1 tablespoon chopped fresh basil leaves *or* 1 teaspoon dried basil
¼–½ teaspoon red pepper flakes, as desired
½ cup (2 ounces) shredded mozzarella cheese
2 tablespoons freshly grated Parmesan cheese, preferably Parmesano-Reggiano

Pound chicken to ½-inch thickness. Combine flour, salt, and pepper in a paper or plastic bag, place chicken in bag and shake to coat with flour mixture. Heat oil in a large skillet over medium-high heat. Add chicken and garlic and cook 3 minutes per side. Reduce heat to medium. Combine spaghetti sauce, basil, and pepper flakes and pour over

chicken
onion + mushroom + garlic + hot pepper
+ wine + stock + tomato sauce, herbs
Return chicken + cheese

chicken. Sprinkle with mozzarella and Parmesan cheeses; cover and cook until chicken is cooked through and cheese has melted, 3 to 4 minutes.

Serving suggestions: Serve with bread sticks and mostaccioli, ziti, or other small pasta tossed with a small amount of additional spaghetti sauce.

PESTO-STUFFED CHICKEN BREASTS

If you love pesto, as my family does, you might make up a big batch and freeze it in small quantities to add to soups, stews, chicken salad sandwiches, and salad dressings. If you are out of fresh pesto, you can find prepared pesto in the imported foods sections of most large supermarkets or specialty stores.

Preparation time: 10 minutes
Cooking time: 10 minutes
Makes 4 servings

2 whole chicken breasts, boned (*not* split or skinned)
⅓ cup pesto (recipe follows)
1 tablespoon melted butter or olive oil
1 tablespoon fresh lemon juice

Run fingers between skin and flesh of chicken to form a pocket. Spread pesto evenly under skin. Combine butter and lemon juice and brush over chicken. Grill or broil 4 to 5 inches from heat source, turning and basting once with remaining butter mixture until chicken is cooked through, about 5 minutes per side. Split each chicken breast in half.

Serving suggestions: Serve with a sliced tomato salad and crusty whole-wheat bread or rolls.

PESTO

Makes ⅓ cup

½ cup packed fresh basil leaves
1 tablespoon toasted pine nuts or walnuts
1 clove garlic
2 tablespoons good quality olive oil
¼ cup freshly grated Parmesan cheese

Combine basil, pine nuts, and garlic in a food processor or blender. Process until fairly smooth, scraping down sides once. With motor running, add oil in a stream; process until smooth. Add cheese; process just until cheese is incorporated.

TARRAGON CHICKEN WITH GORGONZOLA SAUCE

Purchasing small amounts of cheese from a deli counter takes a few minutes longer, but the flavor and quality more than compensate. Imported Gorgonzola cheese has a rich, creamy flavor. If you wish to substitute blue cheese, cut the amount to ¼ cup, as blue cheese has a sharper flavor. I prefer Danish bleu or domestic Maytag blue cheese over prepackaged blue cheese.

Preparation time: 5 minutes
Cooking time: 12 minutes
Makes 4 servings

2 whole chicken breasts, split, boned, and skinned
½ teaspoon salt
¼ teaspoon ground white pepper
2 tablespoons butter or margarine
⅓ cup crumbled Gorgonzola cheese
¼ cup chicken broth
¼ cup heavy cream
1 tablespoon minced fresh tarragon *or* 1 teaspoon dried tarragon

Pound chicken to ½-inch thickness. Sprinkle with salt and pepper. Heat butter in a large skillet over medium-high heat. Cook chicken in butter until cooked through, about 5 minutes per side. Remove chicken from skillet and reduce heat to medium. Add remaining ingredients to skillet and whisk until thickened and well blended. Return chicken to skillet. Spoon sauce over chicken and heat through.

Serving suggestions: Serve with whole-wheat pasta and a steamed green vegetable.

CHICKEN WITH WHITE BEANS, SUN-DRIED TOMATOES, AND ROSEMARY

From the northwest region of Tuscany comes this hearty dish, which is reminiscent of a chicken cassoulet but is prepared in a fraction of the time. Cannellini beans (white kidney beans) can be found in the Italian section of large supermarkets.

Preparation time: 5 minutes
Cooking time: 15 minutes
Makes 4 servings

1 medium yellow onion, coarsely chopped
3 cloves garlic, minced
2 tablespoons olive oil
1 pound boneless, skinless chicken breasts or chicken tenders
1 teaspoon ground coriander
½ teaspoon salt
¼ teaspoon freshly ground black pepper
1 19-ounce can cannellini beans *or* 1 16-ounce can great northern beans, drained
½ cup chicken broth
⅓ cup chopped, drained sun-dried tomatoes in oil
1½ tablespoons coarsely chopped fresh rosemary *or* 1½ teaspoons dried, crushed rosemary
Freshly ground black pepper to taste

Cook onion, garlic, and oil in a large skillet over medium-high heat until softened, about 3 minutes. Meanwhile, cut chicken into 1½-inch pieces. Sprinkle chicken with coriander, salt, and pepper. Add chicken to skillet and cook, stirring constantly, for 1 minute. Add beans, broth, tomatoes, and rosemary. Cover and simmer until chicken is cooked through, 8 to 10 minutes. Serve in shallow bowls with pepper.

Serving suggestions: Serve with crusty Italian bread and a salad of romaine lettuce, black olives, and red onion rings tossed with vinaigrette dressing.

CHICKEN AND PEPPERS
IN BALSAMIC VINEGAR GLAZE

The best balsamic vinegar comes from the Moderno region of Italy. It is aged and produced like sherry and may be found next to the red wine vinegar on the supermarket shelf. Red and yellow bell peppers have become available year-round, so you may serve this colorful dish during any season. Green bell pepper may be substituted for either the red or yellow pepper, but the flavor of the dish will not be as sweet.

Preparation time: 3 minutes
Cooking time: 14 minutes
Makes 4 servings

2 whole chicken breasts, split and boned (skinned if desired)
Salt and freshly ground black pepper to taste
2 tablespoons butter or margarine
1 small red bell pepper
1 small yellow bell pepper
2 cloves garlic
3 tablespoons balsamic vinegar
2 teaspoons honey

Pound chicken to ½-inch thickness. Sprinkle with salt and pepper to taste. Heat butter in a large skillet. Add chicken and cook over medium-high heat until cooked through, 4 to 5 minutes per side. Meanwhile, cut peppers lengthwise into thin strips. Mince garlic. Transfer chicken to a serving platter and keep warm. Add peppers and garlic to drippings in the skillet and cook until peppers are tender, about 4 minutes, stirring frequently. Spoon peppers over chicken. Add vinegar and honey to skillet; stir with wooden spoon until reduced to a glaze, about 1 minute. Spoon evenly over chicken and peppers.

Serving suggestions: Serve with baked potatoes and casaba or cantaloupe wedges.

GERMAN BROILED CHICKEN WITH MUSTARD CRUMBS

German Düsseldorf mustard gives this dish a tangy flavor, but Dijon or spicy brown mustard may be substituted.

Preparation time: 3 minutes
Cooking time: 12 minutes
Makes 4 servings

2 whole chicken breasts, split and boned (skinned if desired)
1 tablespoon olive oil
Salt and freshly ground black pepper to taste
4 tablespoons Düsseldorf or Dijon-style mustard, divided
½ cup fresh bread crumbs, preferably sourdough or rye (see Note)
1 tablespoon dry sherry

Pound chicken to ½-inch thickness. Place on a broiler pan, skin-side down. Brush lightly with oil and sprinkle with salt and pepper. Broil 4 inches from heat source for 5 minutes. Brush 1 tablespoon of the mustard over chicken. Sprinkle with half of the bread crumbs and broil for 1 minute or until crumbs are deep golden brown. Turn chicken over, brush lightly with oil, and sprinkle with salt and pepper. Broil for 4 minutes or until chicken is cooked through. Brush 1 tablespoon mustard over chicken and sprinkle with remaining bread crumbs. Broil for 1 minute or until crumbs are deep golden brown. Combine remaining 2 tablespoons mustard and sherry to serve as a dipping sauce.

Note: To make fresh bread crumbs, process torn sliced bread in a food processor or blender.

Serving suggestions: Serve with sliced pickled beets, sauerkraut, and boiled potatoes.

CHICKEN PAPRIKASH

Hungarian paprika has much more flavor than the domestic variety. Tins of sweet and hot Hungarian paprika are readily available in large supermarkets or specialty food stores. Paprika has a high oil content, so be sure to store it in the refrigerator to avoid spoilage. For a spicier dish, add an additional ¼ teaspoon of hot Hungarian paprika to the seasonings.

Preparation time: 5 minutes
Cooking time: 12 minutes
Makes 4 servings

2 whole chicken breasts, split, boned, and skinned
1 tablespoon paprika, preferably sweet Hungarian
½ teaspoon salt
¼ teaspoon freshly ground black pepper
1 tablespoon olive oil
½ cup well-drained sauerkraut
½ cup sour cream
Paprika as garnish (optional)

Heat oven to 425°F. Pound chicken to ½-inch thickness and sprinkle evenly with paprika, salt, and pepper. Heat oil in a large oven-proof skillet over medium-high heat. Cook chicken in oil 3 minutes per side. Top evenly with sauerkraut and spread sour cream evenly over sauerkraut. Sprinkle with additional paprika, if desired. Transfer skillet to oven and bake uncovered for 6 minutes or until chicken is cooked through.

Serving suggestions: Serve with dark rye bread and steamed baby carrots.

POLISH CHICKEN WITH SOUR CREAM-DILL GRAVY

My Polish housekeeper, Donna, is an excellent cook. When I asked her how she prepares chicken she recited a long, involved recipe which she said was her children's favorite. Here is a simplified version of the delicious dish.

Preparation time: 4 minutes
Cooking time: 14 minutes
Makes 4 servings

2 tablespoons butter or margarine
1 small yellow onion or 4 medium shallots, chopped fine
2 whole chicken breasts, split, boned, and skinned
½ teaspoon salt
¼ teaspoon freshly ground black pepper
¼ cup sour cream
1 tablespoon chopped fresh dill *or* 1 teaspoon dried dill
Sprig dill as garnish (optional)

Heat butter in a large skillet. Add onion and cook over medium heat for 4 minutes. Meanwhile, pound chicken to ½-inch thickness and sprinkle with salt and pepper. Push onion to the edge of the skillet and add chicken. Cook until chicken is lightly browned and cooked through, about 4 minutes per side. Transfer chicken to a serving plate. Remove the skillet from heat and stir in sour cream and dill. Pour mixture over chicken. Garnish with a dill sprig, if desired.

Serving suggestions: Serve with pureed boiled parsnips and carrots glazed with brown sugar and mustard.

CHICKEN MARSALA

The flavor of marsala wine lives up to its reputation of making everything better. Having a bottle on the shelf means you always have a quick flavor enhancer for deglazing the sauté skillet.

Preparation time: 8 minutes
Cooking time: 10 minutes
Makes 4 servings

2 whole chicken breasts, split, boned, and skinned
1 egg, beaten
½ cup seasoned dry bread crumbs
3 tablespoons butter or margarine, divided
2 cloves garlic, minced
¼ cup chicken broth
¼ cup dry marsala wine
Freshly ground black pepper to taste

Pound chicken to ½-inch thickness. Dip in beaten egg and dredge lightly in bread crumbs. Heat 2 tablespoons of the butter in a large skillet. Add chicken and garlic and cook over medium-high heat until chicken is browned and cooked through, about 4 minutes per side. Transfer chicken to a serving platter. Add broth and wine to the skillet and cook over high heat, stirring constantly, until sauce has reduced to a glaze, about 2 minutes. Remove from heat and swirl in remaining tablespoon butter. Pour sauce over chicken and sprinkle with pepper to taste.

Serving suggestions: Serve with your favorite pasta tossed with extra-virgin olive oil, a dash of red pepper flakes, and freshly grated Parmesan cheese.

CHICKEN PAELLA

Paella is the traditional dish of Spain. Its rich color and distinctive flavor come from saffron, an expensive but delicious spice sold in thread or ground form. Turmeric will give the rice a pretty golden color but will not add as much flavor. American basmati rice, sometimes called aromatic or popcorn rice, is now readily available in supermarkets throughout the country.

Preparation time: 1 minute
Cooking time: 19 minutes
Makes 4 servings

1 cup chicken broth
1 8-ounce can stewed tomatoes
1 cup aromatic or American basmati rice
1 pound boneless, skinless chicken breasts or thighs
2 cloves garlic, minced
1 teaspoon salt
½ teaspoon ground saffron or turmeric
¼ teaspoon cayenne pepper
½ pound medium shrimp *or* 8 large live mussels
½ cup frozen or drained canned peas
¼ cup coarsely chopped cilantro or parsley (optional)

Combine broth, tomatoes, and rice in a large skillet. Cover skillet, place over high heat, and bring to a boil. Reduce heat to medium. While the rice cooks, cut chicken into 1½-inch pieces and toss with garlic, salt, saffron, and cayenne pepper. Stir into rice mixture and cover and simmer for 8 minutes. While the mixture simmers, peel and devein shrimp or scrub mussels well. Stir shrimp or mussels and peas into rice mixture. Cover and continue to simmer until shrimp are opaque or mussels are opened, chicken is cooked through, and liquid is absorbed by rice, about 7 minutes. Sprinkle with cilantro, if desired.

Serving suggestions: Serve with a spinach salad with red onion rings and crusty French or Italian bread.

BASQUE CHICKEN

The Basque region of the Pyrenees gives the world the best of two countries, Spain and France. Bouquet garni is a combination of nine savory seasonings. It is found in the spice section of the supermarket. Fines herbes, another seasoning blend, may be substituted.

Preparation time: 5 minutes
Cooking time: 15 minutes
Makes 4 servings

2 tablespoons flour
½ teaspoon salt
½ teaspoon bouquet garni seasoning blend
½ teaspoon freshly ground black pepper
1 pound boneless, skinless chicken thighs or breasts
2 tablespoons olive oil
1 small yellow onion, cut into thin wedges
2 cloves garlic, quartered
1 16-ounce can Italian-style plum tomatoes, undrained
⅓ cup pitted green olives
¼ cup dry red wine
1 to 2 tablespoons drained sliced pickled jalapeño
    peppers, as desired
¼ cup diced salami or prosciutto (optional)

Combine flour and seasonings in plastic bag. Add chicken and shake to coat. Heat oil in a large skillet over medium-high heat. Add chicken, onion, and garlic. Cook for 2 minutes; turn. Add remaining ingredients except salami and bring to a boil. Reduce heat and simmer uncovered for 10 to 12 minutes or until chicken is cooked through and sauce has thickened, stirring frequently. Sprinkle with salami, if desired.

Serving suggestions: Serve with orzo, a rice-shaped pasta, or brown or white rice and crusty Italian bread.

INDEX